COLORING PLUS ACTIVITIES

The Bible Teaches Me

Publisher	Arthur L. Miley
Vice President & Editor	Carolyn Passig Jensen
Art Director	Debbie Birch
Cover Design	Court Patton
Production Director	Barbara Bucher
Production Assistant	Valerie Fetrow
Illustrator	Fran Kizer
Production Artist	Nelson Beltran
Proofreader	Barbara Bucher

Rainbow BOOKS

Copyright © 1996 • Seventh Printing
Rainbow Books • P.O. Box 261129 • San Diego, CA 92196

#RB37161
ISBN 0-937282-46-4

How to Use This Book

These reproducible coloring activities are designed to teach young children biblical principles and stories, and help them apply these important Bible truths to their own lives in practical ways.

These activities are designed to be used in the classroom under the direction of a teacher or leader; they are ideal for Sunday schools, children's church, Vacation Bible Schools, Wednesday night "kid's clubs", and Christian schools.

These coloring activity sheets bring new fun and variety to Bible learning. They are designed to supplement and reinforce Bible stories or lessons or around which to build class sessions. Every activity is created especially for the interests and learning abilities of children ages 4 to 8 years. This book is one of eight similar books which cover many basic, foundational Bible teachings.

This book contains 48 delightful coloring and activity sheets, plus teaching tips and ideas for teachers on how to use the coloring and activity sheets to teach important biblical concepts. All sheets may be reproduced for use with children in Bible-teaching classes.

The coloring and activity sheets in this book are grouped into four thematic chapters. Each chapter begins with two pages of teaching tips which provide the teacher with helpful hints for lesson ideas, instructions for using the coloring and activity sheets, directed conversation to help teach biblical concepts, and much more. (Directed conversation is printed in boldface.) The teaching tips help the teacher relate the spiritual lessons to the children's lives in practical ways they will understand.

Each of the coloring and activity pages in this book includes a picture to color and memory verse on the front side of the sheet. A related activity and another memory verse which teach the children to apply God's Word to their lives, are on the other side of the sheet. Activities include mazes, pictures to color, connect-the-dots, find-and-circle exercises, and much more.

The teacher may chose to reproduce both the coloring sheet *and* the activity sheet, or use either the coloring sheet *or* the activity sheet in one class session. (For most effective learning, however, a copy of both the coloring sheet *and* the corresponding activity sheet should be made for each student.)

First talk with the children about the picture to color, read the caption and teach the memory verse using the teaching tips for the coloring sheet found at the beginning of the chapter. When the children have completed coloring the picture, talk about the corresponding activity sheet, read the caption, teach the memory verse, and guide the children in doing the activity, again using the teaching tips at the beginning of the chapter as your guide. As you work with the children, be sure to relate the biblical lesson to the lives of the children.

The children should also be encouraged to take their coloring and activity sheets home, tell their family what they learned and display the sheets to help them remember the practical application of the lesson. Memory verses may be reviewed in later classes to assure the children really do make the Bible lessons these sheets teach part of their lives.

Crayons or felt-tip markers are all that are required for most activities. Pencils, scissors, construction paper and glue, paste or tape may be used occasionally. The pages in this book are perforated for easy removal of the sheets for copying.

The New King James Version is the biblical reference used through this book, unless noted otherwise.

These coloring activities make it easy to teach important biblical concepts in practical ways children understand and remember.

CONTENTS

The Bible is God's Word

The Bible teaches me about Jesus my Savior
Pages 9 and 10

Coloring Sheet: Talk with the children about Jesus. Who is He? Why did He live on the earth? Emphasize the following points: Jesus is God's Son. Jesus came to live on the earth to tell people about God, His Father and how we can serve God. When we do bad things (sin) it makes Jesus sad. But if we are sorry and ask Him, Jesus will forgive us. Jesus is called our Savior, because He will forgive us for our sins when we ask Him. Introduce and learn the Bible verse. Explain the Bible tells us that Jesus is the Christ, our Savior.

Activity Sheet: Before class time, cut one construction paper rectangle 7 1/4 by 5 1/2 inches for each child. Print "Bible" on each. Allow the children to color the picture of Jesus. Read the caption and explain that the Bible tells us many things about Jesus. In your Bible, show the children pre-marked verses about Jesus. Learn the verse together.

Help the children tape or glue the construction paper rectangle to the picture and open the "Bible" to see the picture of Jesus.

The Bible teaches me how to worship God
Pages 11 and 12

Talk to the children about what it means to worship God. Ask the children to name places we can worship God. Make sure the children understand we can worship God anywhere, but one reason we come to church is to worship.

Coloring Sheet: As the children color, talk about things we do at church to worship God. Point out that reading the Bible and attending church services (as shown in the illustration) are ways we can worship God. Learn the verse together; explain that prayer (bowing down) is another way we worship God.

Activity Sheet: Help the children connect the dots in order to complete the drawing of a church building. Help the children learn the verse. Discuss reasons we should be glad to go to church. Be sure children understand that worshipping God is one reason to be glad to go to church.

The Bible tells me exciting stories of God's love
Pages 13 and 14

Tell the story of Noah's ark, emphasizing God's love in caring for Noah, his family and the animals.

Coloring Sheet: Distribute the coloring sheet and read the caption. Say, **God's Word has many other stories about God's Love,** and show the children the pre-marked passages of some familiar stories such as Daniel in the lion's den, Baby Moses, Joseph, Baby Jesus, etc. Then say, **God's Word is true. These stories really happened. That is what our memory verse tells us.** Help the children learn the verse.

Activity Sheet: Help the children identify the stories pictured and direct them to draw lines to the correct words. Then let selected children tell the stories to the rest of the class. Say, **God wants us to remember the stories in His Word. Let's learn our memory verse together.** Guide the children in learning the verse.

The Bible helps me share God's love with others
Pages 15 and 16

Talk with the children about what it means to share God's love with others. Help them understand there are many ways we can do this.

Coloring Sheet: Introduce the memory verse and say, **God tells us in the Bible to tell other people about Him. That's what is meant by "preaching the Gospel." We can do this wherever we are.** Talk about ways the children can tell others about Jesus.

Activity Sheet: Help the children understand that our actions are one way people know we love Jesus and are trying to live for Him. Instruct the children to look at each picture and decide if that activity shows people they love Jesus. The children may circle the actions which are pleasing to Jesus and cross out the others. Talk about other actions which show people we love Jesus. Then learn the memory verse, emphasizing that God wants us to obey the Bible by telling others about Him, through our words and our actions.

The Bible helps me pray to God
Page 17 and 18

Talk with the children about prayer. Be sure they understand that prayer is talking to God and that they can pray to God and tell Him anything at anytime and from anyplace.

Coloring Sheet: Point out that one good time to pray is at bedtime (as shown in the picture). Emphasize that we should have a special time each day when we talk to God and read the Bible. Introduce the verse and say, **God's Word tells us how to pray to Him. It also says that God will hear our prayer when we pray (call) to Him.** Learn the verse together.

Activity Sheet: Emphasize again that we can talk to God or Jesus anytime. Discuss each of the different situations shown and help the children pick out two times that they have prayed to Jesus. Then help them select two additional times they will pray this week. Learn the verse. Say, **God wants us to talk to Him anytime. God likes to hear our prayers.**

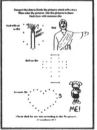

The Bible is God's message to me
Pages 19 and 20

Talk about the Bible. Help the children understand that it is God's very special message for us.

Coloring Sheet: Help the children think about why the Bible is so important. Then say, **God says we are to learn and remember what God tells us in the Bible. Our memory verse tells us why we are to do this. It says it is so we will not sin against God.** Help the children understand how learning from the Bible will help them live the way God wants them to.

Activity Sheet: Guide the children in connecting the dots to create separate pictures of a Bible, a cross and a heart. Help the children to read the picture message. Tell the children that this is the story the Bible tells us. Then present the plan of salvation simply and give the children opportunity to respond. Introduce the verse by saying, **The Bible tells us about Jesus and that He died so we can be forgiven for our sins. That is what our memory verse tells us too.**

The Bible teaches me about Jesus my Savior

(The Scriptures) are written that you may believe
that Jesus is the Christ.

John 20:31

The Bible tells us about Jesus. Color the picture of Jesus. Then cut out a construction paper cover the same size as the book and tape it to the side of the book. Print BIBLE on the cover. Open the "Bible" to see Jesus!

Tape or Glue Cover Here

The Scriptures . . . testify of (Jesus).

John 5:39

The Bible teaches me how to worship God

O come, let us worship and bow down:
Psalm 95:6 KJV

Connect the dots to finish the picture of one
place we can worship God. Then color the picture.

I was glad when they said to me, "Let us go
into the house of the Lord."

Psalm 122:1

The Bible tells me exciting stories of God's love

Your word is truth.
John 17:17

Draw a line to match the pictures of Bible stories on the left to the names of the people in the story on the right.
Then tell one of the stories to a friend or your teacher.

Baby Moses

Noah

Daniel

I will not forget Your word.

Psalm 119:16

The Bible helps me share God's love with others

"Go into all the world and preach the gospel"
Mark 16:15

Circle the ways you can tell others about Jesus.
Cross out the ways which are a bad witness.

Blessed are those who hear the word of God and keep it!
Luke 11:28

The Bible helps me pray to God

The Lord will hear when I call to Him.
Psalm 4:3

You can pray to Jesus anytime. Put an X near each picture showing a time when you have prayed to Jesus. Then choose two new times when you will pray this week. Put a star beside them.

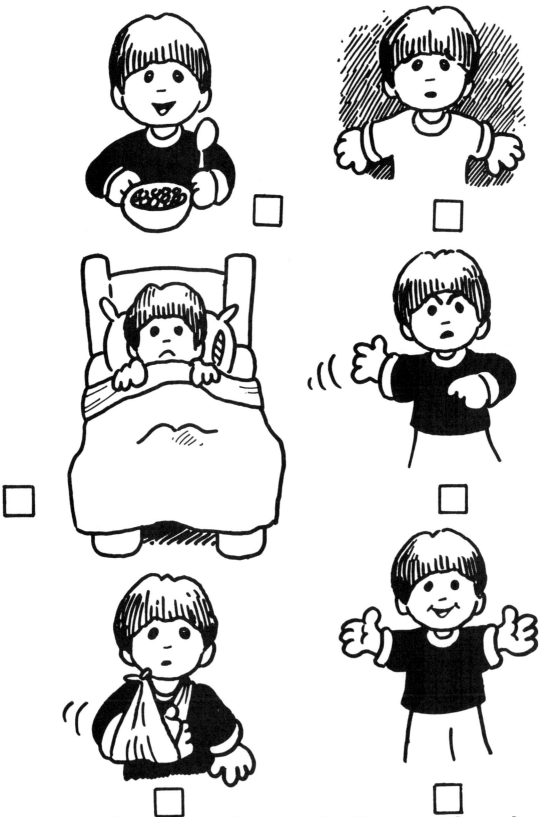

Evening and morning and at noon I will pray, and cry aloud,
Psalm 55:17

The Bible is God's message to me

I have hidden Your word in my heart
that I might not sin against You.
Psalm 119:11 NIV

Connect the dots to finish the pictures which tell a story.
Then color the pictures. Use the pictures to share
God's love with someone else.

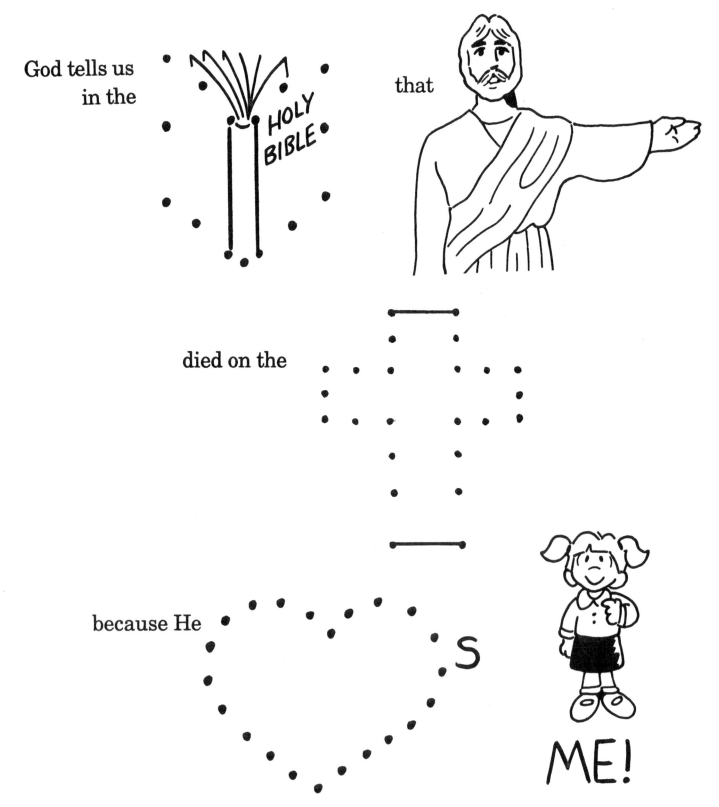

God tells us in the [HOLY BIBLE] that [picture of Jesus]

died on the [cross dots]

because He [heart dots] 'S [picture of girl] ME!

Christ died for our sins according to the Scriptures,
1 Corinthians 15:3

The Bible Teaches Me about My Friend Jesus

Jesus is my friend. I talk to Him each day in prayer
Pages 23 and 24

Ask the children to tell your what it means to talk to Jesus in prayer. Discuss things which we can talk to Jesus about. Emphasize that we can talk to Jesus about anything. Talk about what it means to have Jesus as our friend. If desired, present the plan of salvation simply and offer the children an opportunity to accept Jesus as their own friend.

Coloring Sheet: Introduce the memory verse by saying, **The Bible tells us that when we talk to Jesus in prayer, He will hear us. That is one reason I like to talk to Jesus, because I know He hears me.**

Activity Sheet: Reiterate that we can talk to Jesus in prayer about anything. Talk about the pictures and help the children to choose and color pictures of things they can talk to Jesus about. Of course, all pictures should be colored. Say, **Not only can we talk to Jesus about anything, we can talk to Jesus anytime.** Then learn the memory verse.

Jesus is my friend. He protects me from danger
Pages 25 and 26

Ask the children to name things they are afraid of or that might be dangerous. Ask them if they think Jesus can protect them from these things. Emphasize that Jesus is with us all the time, even when we are asleep, and that He is watching over us.

Coloring Sheet: As the children color, learn the memory verse with them. Take turns saying the verse as follows: Teacher: "So do not fear," Children: "For I am with you."

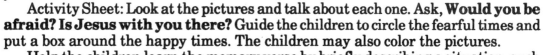

Activity Sheet: Look at the pictures and talk about each one. Ask, **Would you be afraid? Is Jesus with you there?** Guide the children to circle the fearful times and put a box around the happy times. The children may also color the pictures.

Help the children learn the memory verse by briefly describing a situation, such as, **When I lose my mother in a big store....** The children answer with the memory verse, "I will never leave you nor forsake you."

Jesus is my friend and my Savior. He forgives my sins
Pages 27 and 28

Talk about what sin is. Have the children name actions which are sin.

Coloring Sheet: Talk about what the boy in the picture is doing. **Is this a sin? What will Jesus do about our sins if we ask Him?** Present the plan of salvation and offer the children a chance to ask Jesus to forgive their sins. Then ask, **What did Jesus do for you just now?** Learn the memory verse to help the children remember that Jesus forgives sins.

Activity Sheet: Discuss each picture together. Be sure the children can identify what is the sinful or wrong activity in each picture. Help the children find pictures of the things they have done wrong. Emphasize that sins make Jesus sad. Say, **Our memory verse tells us that Jesus died for our sins. He died and came alive again so our sins could be forgiven.** Offer the children time to ask Jesus to forgive them.

Jesus is my friend. I know He loves me
Pages 29 and 30

Help the children to understand Jesus' love. Tell them Jesus loves them. Say, **The Bible tells us Jesus loves us, so we know that He really does.** Then sing the chorus, "Jesus Loves Me." Learn the memory verse on the Coloring Sheet. Talk to the children about what it means to love someone.

Activity Sheet: Talk about the things Jesus does for us because He loves us. Center your emphasis on Jesus' presence and protection of us. As the children do the maze, talk about the various hazards and warn the children about busy streets, dangerous rivers and streams, talking to strangers, and other dangers. Learn the the memory verse together. Ask the children to tell you what they should do if they are afraid. (Trust in Jesus.)

Jesus is my friend. He is with me all the time — even in the dark
Pages 31 and 32

Ask the children to name unusual places they have been. Ask, **Was Jesus with you, Jason, when you went up in the airplane? Was Jesus with you, Aimee, when you went in the submarine at Disneyland?** Assure the children Jesus is with them everywhere. Say, **Jesus is with you always, even in places where you might be afraid — like in the dark or other places.** Learn the memory verse on the Coloring Sheet together.

Activity Sheet: Tell the children, **Although we can't see Him, Jesus is beside us and with us all the time.** Help the children to draw a picture of themselves next to the picture of Jesus. Suggest the children take their picture home and put it up in their room to remind them of Jesus' promise in the memory verse, "I am with you and will watch over you."

Jesus is my friend. Someday I can go to live with Him in heaven
Pages 33 and 34

Talk to the children about heaven and how wonderful it will be. Say, **Jesus has prepared a very special place where we can live forever if we have accepted Jesus as our Savior.**

Coloring Sheet: Talk about the characteristics of heaven. Help the children to color heaven using gold crayons or markers, or glue on glitter and sequins. Learn the memory verse together.

Activity Sheet: Introduce the Activity Sheet and memory verse by saying, **Sometimes it's hard to live for Jesus, but Jesus is always with us and He has promised to help us and show us what to do.** The children may complete the maze to find the path to heaven. Explain that the only way to get to heaven is to accept Jesus as Savior. Present the plan of salvation and give the children an opportunity to respond.

Jesus is my friend. I talk to Him each day in prayer

The LORD will hear when I call to Him.

Psalm 4:3

You can talk to Jesus in prayer about anything. He is always listening. Color the pictures which show some things you can talk to Jesus about.

Evening and morning and at noon I will pray

Psalm 55:17

Jesus is my friend. He protects me from danger

So do not fear, for I am with you;

Isaiah 41:10 NIV

Jesus is with you all the time. Circle the times you would be
afraid, but Jesus is with you. Put a box around the happy times.
Jesus is with you then too.

"I will never leave you nor forsake you."
Hebrews 13:5

Jesus is my friend and my Savior. He forgives my sins

You are kind and forgiving, O Lord,
Psalm 86:5 NIV

Jesus loves us and will forgive us when we do wrong. Find and circle the pictures below which show something you have done wrong. Have you asked Jesus to forgive you? Ask Him now. Then color the pictures.

Christ died for our sins.
1 Corinthians 15:3

Jesus is my friend. I know He loves me

For God so loved the world,
John 3:16 KJV

Because Jesus loves you, He is with you all the time and can protect you from dangers and care for you. Find the way home past dangers from which Jesus can protect you.

Whenever I am afraid, I will trust in You.
Psalm 56:3

Jesus is my friend. He is with me all the time – even in the dark

"I will never leave you nor forsake you."
Hebrews 13:5

Jesus is with you all the time, caring for you and protecting you. Draw a picture of yourself next to Jesus. Then color the picture.

I am with you and will watch over you.

Genesis 28:15 NIV

Jesus is my friend. Someday I can go to live with Him in heaven

I will dwell in the house of the LORD forever.
Psalm 23:6

Jesus promised to guide us and be with us. When we follow Him, He will lead us and someday we can go to live with Him in heaven. Find the right path to heaven in the maze below.

You guide me . . . and afterward You will take me into glory.
Psalm 73:24 NIV

The Bible Teaches Me to Obey God

I obey God when I am kind and helpful to others
Pages 37 and 38

Ask the children to tell what it means to be kind and helpful to others.

Coloring Sheet: Talk about the picture on the Coloring Sheet. Ask, **What happened? What would you do in this situation?** Then say, **God tells us in the Bible to be kind to one another. When we do something kind and helpful, we are obeying God.** Help the children to learn the memory verse.

Activity Sheet: Talk about each picture and allow the children to choose and circle the pictures which show children who are pleasing God and cross out the other pictures. Introduce the memory verse by saying, **In the Bible, Jesus tells us to love each other like Jesus loves us. One way we show our love for others is by being kind and helpful.** Learn the verse and then allow each child to name one kind and helpful way they will show their love for someone this week.

I obey God by helping my parents
Pages 39 and 40

Coloring Sheet: Discuss the picture and ask the children to name things they can do in obedience to their parents. Ask, **How should you act when your parents ask you to do something?** Then introduce the memory verse by saying, **The Bible tells us to obey our parents in the Lord.** Learn the memory verse together. As the children color, cite various situations, such as, **Lani, what should you do when you mother asks you to sweep the floor?** The child should answer "Obey my parents in the Lord."

Activity Sheet: Talk to the children about keeping their rooms and toys neat and put away. Show the children how to draw a line from the objects on the left to the place where it belongs on the right. Then say, **Sometimes we don't want to do what our parents ask. The Bible says the Lord is our helper. What should we do when we feel like disobeying?** Allow the children time to discuss this. Then say, **When we feel like disobeying, we should ask the Lord to help us to do what is right.** Learn the memory verse together.

I obey God by worshipping at church
Pages 41 and 42

Coloring Sheet: Ask the children to tell what is happening in the picture. Say, **God is happy when we come to church each week. Church is one place we can worship God.** Then ask the children to tell how they should feel about coming to church. Say, **The Bible tells us it is good to be happy to go to church. Were you happy to come to church today?** Learn the memory verse together.

Activity Page: Talk with the children about proper behavior in church and why we act properly in reverence to God. Then talk about some of the things we do at church. Introduce the memory verse by saying, **The Bible tells us some of the things we are to do in church. It says we are to "enter with thanksgiving and praise." What are somethings we do in church to show our thanksgiving and praise to God?** Discuss each picture and ask the children to circle those which show something they should do in church and cross out the others.

I obey God when I forgive others
Pages 43 and 44

Coloring Sheet: Ask the children, **How would you feel if your friend was playing with your favorite toy and he or she broke it? What should you do?** Pass out the coloring sheet and explain that the girl on the right is forgiving the other girl who broke the first girl's doll. Explain what it means to forgive, and then say, **The Bible tells us to be kind to each other and forgive each other.** Learn the verse together.

Activity Sheet: Before class time, prepare one construction paper frame for each child by cutting a 6 inch by 7 inch rectangle out of a sheet of construction paper. As the children color, discuss situations in which the children should be forgiving of others. Learn (or review) the memory verse together also. When the children have completed coloring, help them to tape or glue the Activity Sheet to the back of the construction paper frame so the picture shows through the frame. Encourage the children to put their picture up at home to remind them to be kind and forgiving.

I obey God by talking to Him in prayer each day
Pages 45 and 46

Tell the children, **Prayer is talking to God. God wants us to talk to Him each day in prayer.**

Coloring Sheet: As the children color, ask them to name times or places they can talk to God, and/or to name things about which they can talk to God. Then say, **The Bible tells us we can pray to God anytime of the day — in the morning, at night, at lunch time or when its time to go to bed.** Then learn the memory verse together.

Activity Sheet: Guide the children in connecting the dots to complete the picture of a car. Say, **This is one place we can talk to God. Can you think of other places when you can talk to God?** Give each child a chance to name other places where they can pray. Then introduce the memory verse by saying, **It's nice to know that no matter where we are, God will hear us when we pray.**

I obey God by telling the truth
Pages 47 and 48

Coloring Sheet: Ask the children, **What should you do if you broke your mother's pretty vase and she asked who did it?** Allow time for answers, then say, **God wants us to always tell the truth. The Bible says, "Do not lie to one another."** Learn the verse together.

Activity Sheet: Talk about each picture and, if desired, other situations where the children might be tempted to not tell the truth. After each, emphasize that we should always tell the truth and encourage the children to draw a happy face beside each picture to indicate they would tell the truth. Introduce and learn the memory verse; explain that to "bear false witness" is to tell a lie and God tells us not to do this.

I obey God when I am kind and helpful to others

Be ye kind one to another,
Ephesians 4:32 KJV

Circle the pictures showing children who are pleasing God.
Cross out the ones who are doing something which makes God sad.

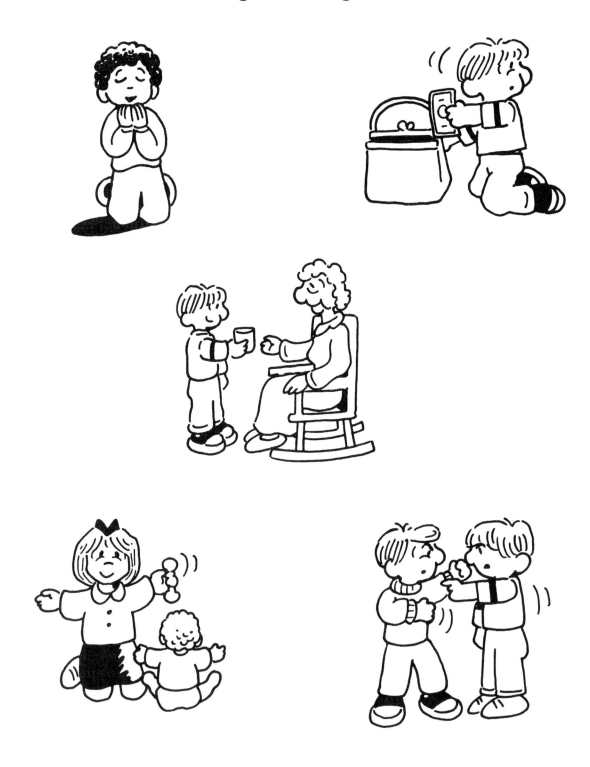

Love one another; as I have loved you,
John 13:34

I obey God by helping my parents

Children, obey your parents in the Lord,
Ephesians 6:1

I can help my parents by putting things away where they belong.
Draw a line from each thing on the left to the place where it belongs.

The Lord is my helper;
Hebrews 13:6

I obey God by **worshipping** at church

I was glad when they said to me,
"Let us go into the house of the Lord."

Psalm 122:1

Circle the things that you should do in church.
Cross out the things which you should not do.

Enter into His gates with thanksgiving,
And into His courts with praise.

Psalm 100:4

I obey God when I forgive others

Be kind to one another, . . . forgiving one another.
Ephesians 4:32

God is pleased when we obey Him by being kind and forgiving to others. Color this pretty picture and make a frame for it. Then put it up in your room to remind you to be kind and forgiving.

To make a frame for this page, cut a 6 inch by 7 inch rectangle out of the center of a sheet of construction paper. Tape or glue this page to the back of the construction paper frame so the picture shows through the frame.

I obey God by talking to Him in prayer each day

Evening and morning and at noon I will pray,
Psalm 55:17

We can talk to God anywhere. Connect the dots to show one place we can talk to God. Then think of some other places where you can talk to God too. Now color the picture.

The LORD will hear when I call to Him.

Psalm 4:3

I obey God by telling the truth

Do not lie to one another,
Colossians 3:9

Sometimes we make mistakes or have accidents, but
we should always tell the truth no matter what.
Draw a happy face beside each picture if you would tell the truth.

You shall not bear false witness.
Exodus 20:16

The Bible Teaches Me How to Live

The Bible teaches me that Jesus loves me
Pages 51 and 52

Talk with the children about Jesus' love for them. Ask them to name ways we know Jesus loves us. If desired, you may also talk about ways we can show Jesus we love Him.

Coloring Sheet: Say, **The Bible tells us Jesus loves us, so we know He really does.** Then sing the chorus, "Jesus Love Me." Introduce the memory verse by saying, **The Bible say we love Jesus because He loved us first.** Then learn the verse together.

Activity Sheet: Emphasize to the children that Jesus loves them and is with them all the time, even though they can't see Him. Direct each child to connect the broken line to complete the picture of Jesus and to draw his or her face on the appropriate child next to Jesus, and a friend's face on the other figure. In teaching the memory verse, you may wish to present the plan of salvation and tell the children, **Jesus loves us so much that if we believe on Him and accept Him as Savior, we can have everlasting life with Him in heaven.**

The Bible teaches me to tell others about Jesus
Pages 53 and 54

Coloring Sheet: Ask the children to tell what is happening in the picture. Then say, **The boy on the left is inviting the other boy to church. That is one way we can tell others about Jesus.** Talk about other ways we can tell others about Jesus. Then say, **These are all ways we can tell others about Jesus. When we tell others about Jesus we are "preaching the Gospel" like our memory verse tells us to do.** Learn the verse together.

Activity Sheet: Read the caption to the children. Then discuss each picture together. Ask the children to tell which of God's commands the children are obeying or disobeying and help them to draw lines from the obedient pictures to the Bible. (This sheet can be an effective review of many of the concepts taught in this book.) Learn the memory verse together. Say, **The Bible says we are blessed if we hear the Word of God and keep it.**

The Bible teaches me to obey my parents
Pages 55 and 56

Coloring Sheet: Say, **The Bible teaches us to obey our parents because it is right.** Learn the memory verse together. Talk about what the boy is doing in the picture and allow the children to name other ways they can obey and help their parents.

Activity Sheet: Emphasize one way the children can help their parents is by keeping their rooms neat and tidy and helping their parents around the house. Direct the children to find and circle all the objects in the picture which need to be put away. The children may color the picture also. Reiterate that when the children obey their parents, they are obeying the Lord. Help the children to learn the memory verse. If time allows, you may talk with the children about how they should respond when they don't want to obey. Say, **We should always obey the Lord.**

The Bible teaches me to be kind and loving to others
Pages 57 and 58

Coloring Sheet: Ask, **Is the little boy in the picture being kind and loving? What is he doing? Could you do this?** Ask the children to name ways they can be kind and loving to other people. Help the children to learn the memory verse. Say, **God tells us to be kind to one another. When we do kind things for other people we are obeying God.**

Activity Sheet: Discuss each picture in turn. Let the children indicate whether each picture shows kind and loving actions or unkind behavior. Then talk about why we should be kind. Say, **The Bible tells us to love one another because love is God's way. We should be kind and loving because God tells us to do so.** Learn the memory verse to reinforce this.

The Bible teaches me that Jesus came to earth to be my Savior
Pages 59 and 60

Coloring Sheet: Tell or review the Christmas story. Then explain, **The Bible tells us that Jesus came to earth to be our Savior. He will forgive our sins and we can someday live with Him in heaven.** Explain the memory verse and learn it together. Present the plan of salvation and offer an opportunity for the children to accept Jesus as Savior.

Activity Sheet: Before class time, cut 3-inch construction paper squares, making four for each child. Print "Bible" on each. Allow the children to color the pictures. Discuss each picture and briefly tell the stories of Jesus which each shows. Say, **The Bible tells us many wonderful stories about Jesus our Savior.** Learn the memory verse together.

Help the children tape or glue a construction paper square to each picture and open the "Bibles" to see the pictures of Jesus.

The Bible teaches me Jesus died on the cross, but came alive again
Pages 61 and 62

Coloring Sheet: Tell or review the Easter story. Tell the children, **Jesus was willing to die to take the punishment for the sins we have done. Because Jesus is God, He came alive again. When we ask Jesus, He will forgive us for the wrong things we do.** Learn the memory verse together. Provide an opportunity for children to ask Jesus to forgive them and to thank Him for taking the punishment for their sins.

Activity Sheet: Talk about why Jesus died on the cross. Say, **Jesus loves us so much that He died on the cross to take the punishment for the wrong things we do.** Learn the memory verse together. Then direct the children to color the dotted sections red. They may color the other sections various colors to create the effect of a stained-glass window. If the children have not done so, give the opportunity for any children to accept Jesus as their Savior.

The Bible teaches me that Jesus loves me

We love Him, because He first loved us.
1 John 4:19

Jesus loves you. Connect the broken lines to show who is your best friend. Draw your face, and the face of a friend next to Jesus. Then color the picture. Use it to tell someone else about Jesus, your best friend.

God so loved the world that . . . whoever believes in Him should . . . have everlasting life.

John 3:16

The Bible teaches me to tell others about Jesus

Go into all the world and preach the gospel
Mark 16:15

The Bible tells us how to live so others will want to know about Jesus too. Draw lines from the Bible to the pictures of children who are doing what the Bible says.

Blessed are those who hear the word of God and keep it!
Luke 11:28

The Bible teaches me to obey my parents

Children, obey your parents, . . . for this is right.
Ephesians 6:1

You can obey Jesus by cleaning up your room when your mother or father asks you. Find and circle all the things that need to be put away.

(I) will obey . . . the Lord
Jeremiah 42:6

The Bible teaches me to be kind and loving to others

Be kind to one another
Ephesians 4:32

Circle the ways that show others we love and care for them.
Cross out the ways that are unkind and wrong.

Let us love one another, for love is of God;

1 John 4:7

The Bible teaches me that Jesus came to earth to be my Savior

Christ Jesus came into the world to save sinners
1 Timothy 1:15

The Bible tells us about Jesus our Savior. Color the pictures, then make a cover for each book and tape it to the side. Print BIBLE on each cover. Open each "Bible" to see Jesus!

The Scriptures . . . testify of (Jesus)

John 5:39

The Bible teaches me Jesus died on the cross, but came alive again

Christ died for our sins . . . and . . . He rose again
1 Corinthians 15:3-4

Color the dotted sections red. Jesus loves and cares for us so much
that He died on the cross so our sins can be forgiven.
Have you asked Jesus to forgive you?

Christ died for us.

Romans 5:8

INDEX